Discover Halloween

by Juliana O'Neil

© 2017 by Juliana O'Neil
ISBN: 978-1-53240-217-3
eISBN: 978-1-53240-218-0
Images licensed from Fotolia.com
All rights reserved.
No portion of this book may be reproduced
without express permission of the publisher.
First Edition
Published in the United States by
Xist Publishing
www.xistpublishing.com
PO Box 61593 Irvine, CA 92602

Halloween is in the fall.

On October 31st, we carve pumpkins.

We put on costumes.

9

We grab our flashlights and go out the front door.

We go from house to house and see our friends.

At the door, we say, "trick or treat."

I got my favorite candy.
Thank you!

Some people wear scary costumes.

Some houses wear scary decorations.

I am not scared.

I know it is fun to pretend.

Halloween is a good night to celebrate.

At home, we sort our candy.

Then, we brush our teeth and say good night.

www.ingramcontent.com/pod-product-compliance
Lightning Source LLC
LaVergne TN
LVHW010021070426
835507LV00001B/30